DRUMMING
THE EASY WAY!
THE BEGINNER'S GUIDE TO PLAYING DRUMS
FOR STUDENTS AND TEACHERS

599271721

BY TOM HAPKE
CD INCLUDES RECORDED DEMONSTRATIONS
OF EVERY EXERCISE AND SOLO

LANE
COMPANY

DRUMMING
THE EASY WAY!
THE BEGINNER'S GUIDE TO PLAYING DRUMS
FOR STUDENTS AND TEACHERS

CD INCLUDES RECORDED DEMONSTRATIONS OF EVERY EXERCISE AND SOLO

Recording Credits: Tom Hapke, Drums

ISBN 978-1-57560-862-4

Visit our website at www.cherrylane.com

INTRODUCTION

Over the course of the last 30 years the drum set has gradually developed into an important, multifaceted solo and ensemble instrument—it is no longer just an accompanying instrument, but an important and essential element of modern music. The musical approach of this book is based on years of teaching experience. The difficulties that many students experience while reading musical notation are minimized through this practical approach. Students want to play the drums, but they do not necessarily want to study the theory of music. Eventually, theoretical knowledge will be indispensable and the method of this book encourages a gradual development of such knowledge. Through the systematic treatment of the various themes in this book, students will gain the necessary security to realize the potential of the exercises. Conscientious practice is indispensable: Each exercise should be practiced until it can be played without mistakes before moving on to the next. If this is done, the book will encourage fruitful learning. The desirable long-term goals of technique—style and flexibility—can only be built on a firm foundation. *Drumming the Easy Way!* is the quickest and most enjoyable way of promoting the interest and developing the foundation of the student.

— Tom Hapke

Various principles are introduced in this book that will make teaching drums significantly easier:

- Clear and large musical print, with only two bars on each system.

- Intensive treatment of each individual drum figure, leading to greater security.

- Drum solos, which follow each exercise, motivate and increase the "fun factor" for students.

- The text is brief to keep the student's attention on the music. Teachers should explain things in their own way.

- Each facing page is arranged so that the left side is related to the right side.

All of these principles have been systematically tested with students of all ages and abilities.

NOTES ON THE AUDIO CD

The enclosed audio CD contains recordings of the music examples in this book. A track number at the top of a page indicates where all the music examples for that page occur on the CD. One measure of clicks precedes each music example. No repeats are taken.

CONTENTS

Part 1

DRUM NOTATION LEGEND

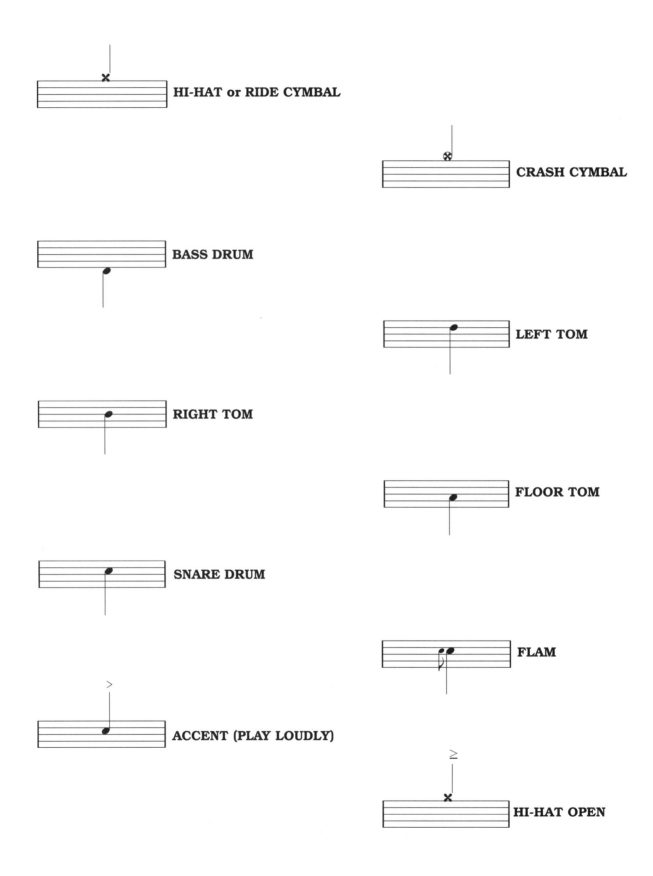

NOTE VALUES

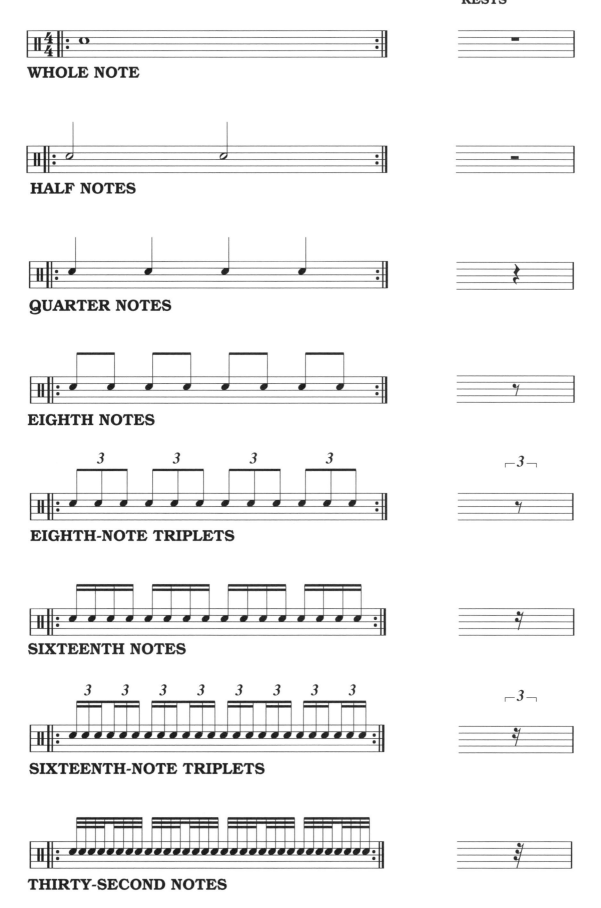

RESTS

WHOLE NOTE

HALF NOTES

QUARTER NOTES

EIGHTH NOTES

EIGHTH-NOTE TRIPLETS

SIXTEENTH NOTES

SIXTEENTH-NOTE TRIPLETS

THIRTY-SECOND NOTES

QUARTER NOTES

(on the Pad)

Track 01

IMPORTANT: This quarter-note exercise should be played at a steady, slow tempo. Count aloud, even during the rests. Practice each staff until it is perfect before going on to the next.

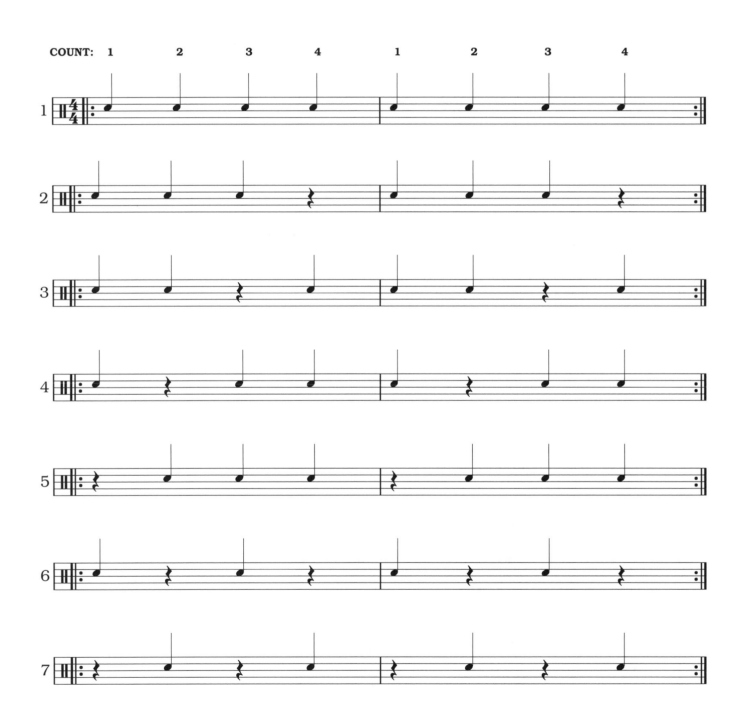

6

SOLO 1

(on the Pad)

Track 02

IMPORTANT: **Play this quarter-note solo without pausing. Again, it is important to count aloud and play at a steady tempo.**

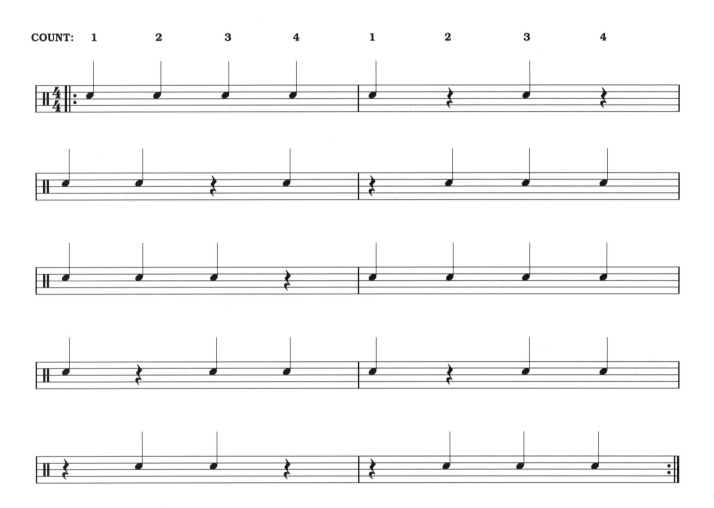

NOTES:

QUARTER-NOTE RHYTHMS
(on the Drums)

Track 03

IMPORTANT: Play Ex. 1 and make certain that your quarter notes have a consistent tone and steady rhythm. After you can play the exercise accurately, the first beat of the bar can be practiced together with the bass drum (Ex. 2). After you've mastered that, practice each exercise on this page one after the other, until you can flow easily from one to the next—while maintaining a steady tempo. Also try playing with the right hand on the ride cymbal instead of the hi-hat.

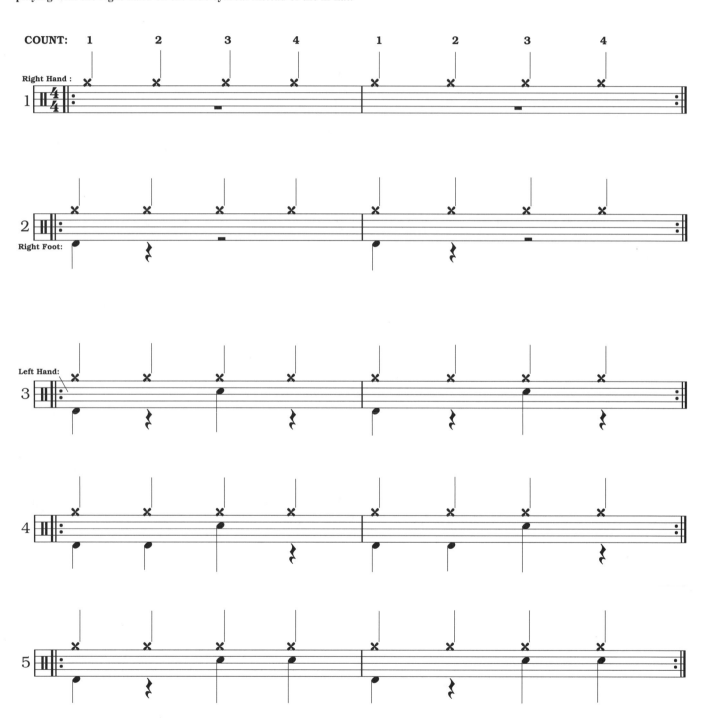

SOLO 1.1

(on the Drums)

Track 04

IMPORTANT: This entire page should be played without pausing. The right hand can play either the hi-hat or the ride cymbal for accompaniment. Practice slowly. Count aloud.

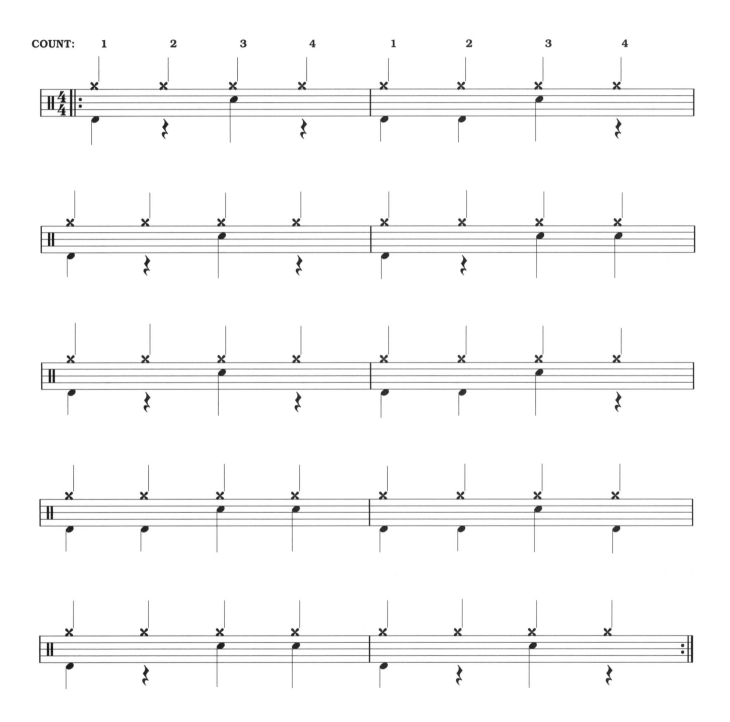

EIGHTH NOTES

(and Quarter Notes)

Track 05

IMPORTANT: **When playing this example, you'll need to count "1 and, 2 and, 3 and, 4 and, *etc.*" (which is notated as "1 + 2 + 3 + 4 +"). Note that the hand order of each exercise consistently alternates—always hand-to-hand. This means that every beat (1, 2, 3, and 4) is played with the right hand, and every "+" with the left hand (or vice-versa!). Maintain the hand-to-hand sticking at all costs. Practice each staff slowly and individually.**

SOLO 2

(on the Pad)

Track 06

IMPORTANT: **Play through this solo without pausing. Pay attention to the hand order (again, it alternates consistently). Keep a steady tempo. Practice slowly at first.**

<u>**NOTES:**</u>

EIGHTH-NOTE GROOVES

(on the Drums)

Track 07

IMPORTANT: When playing these eighth-note grooves we employ a method of counting ("1 and, 2 and, 3 and, 4 and, *etc.*") that is used throughout the book, while at the same time we learn the most typical rhythms of rock and pop drumming. Accompany each exercise once with the hi-hat and once with the ride cymbal. Play slowly. Count aloud. Practice each staff individually.

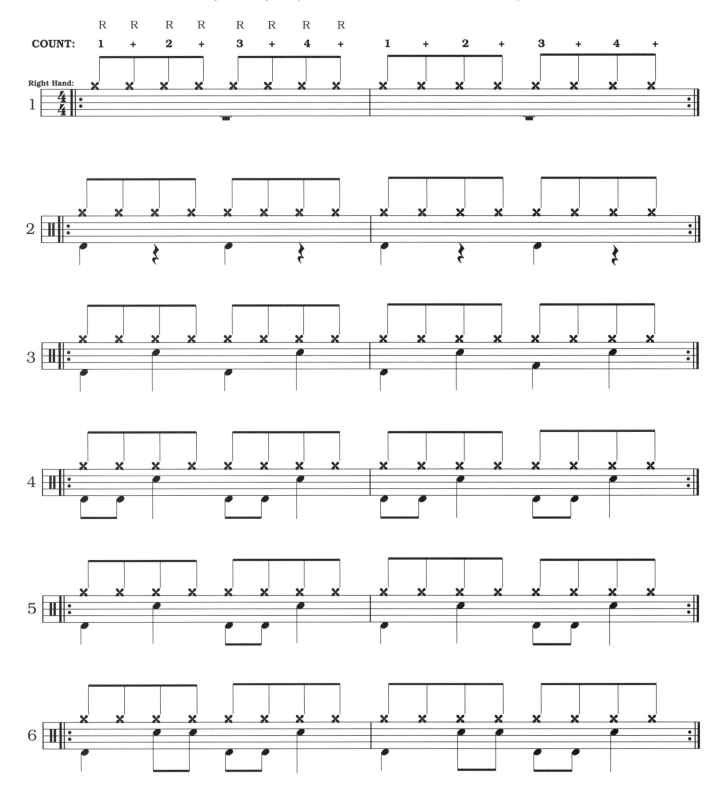

FILLS ON THE DRUMS

(Eighth Notes)

Track 08

IMPORTANT: These examples, on the drums, are *fills* and should be practiced in the same manner as the previous exercises on the pad. The hand order remains the same. This exercise should be played only with the hands—don't add your feet yet. It is very important to play slowly and count aloud.

EIGHTH-NOTE FILLS
(with Crash Cymbal)

Track 09

IMPORTANT: Now we will begin using the crash cymbal. The crash cymbal is always played exactly together with the bass drum. Striking one instrument slightly before the other is undesirable, as the punctuation we intended will be lost. Play slowly. Count aloud. Practice each staff individually.

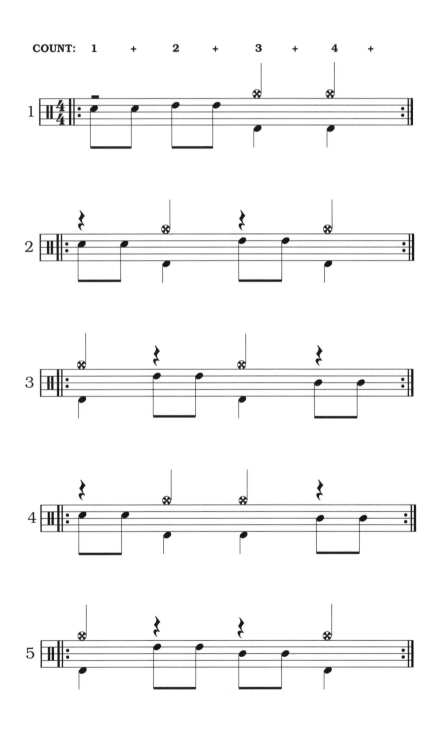

14

EIGHTH-NOTE GROOVES

(with Crash Cymbal)

IMPORTANT: Here, for the first time, the crash cymbal is used as part of the groove. The accompaniment can be played once with the hi-hat and once with the ride cymbal. Play slowly at first. Count aloud. Play each staff individually.

NOTES:

GROOVES AND FILLS

(Eighth Notes)

Track 11

IMPORTANT: Now eighth-note grooves are combined with eighth-note fills. Count evenly and continuously to successfully incorporate the fill into the flow of the groove. Play slowly. Count aloud. Practice each staff individually.

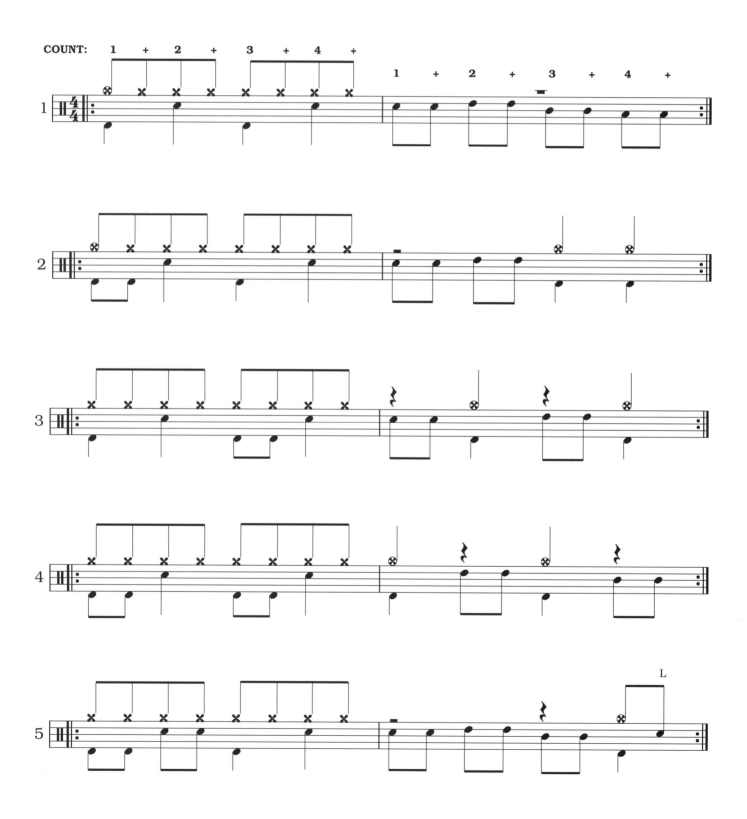

SOLO 2.1

(on the Drums)

Track 12

IMPORTANT: This eighth-note solo should be played without pausing between staves. Play slowly. Count aloud. Practice each staff individually.

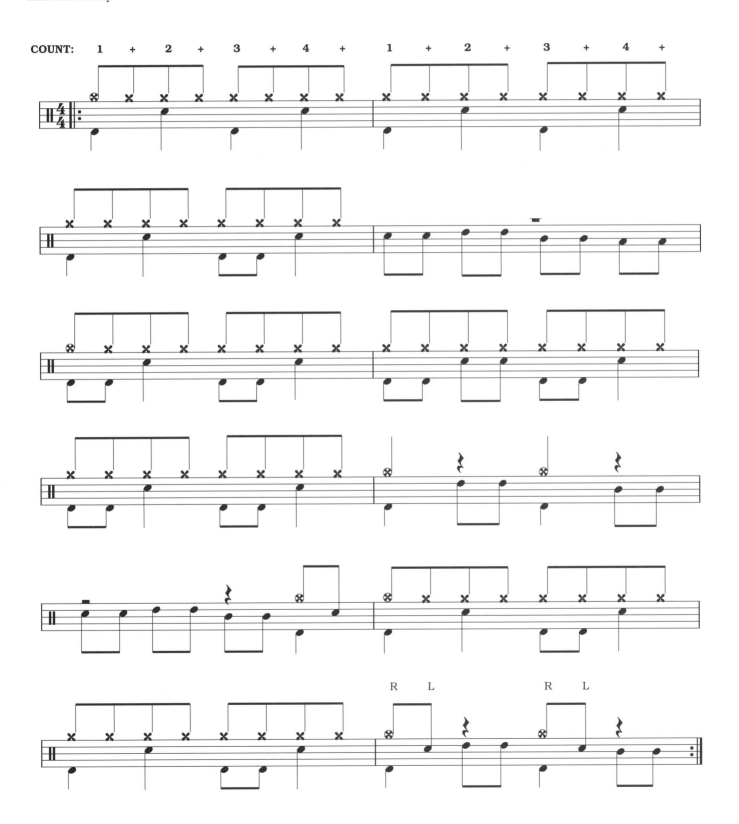

EIGHTH NOTES

(with Eighth Rests)

Track 13

IMPORTANT: Don't forget to count during the rests. Pay attention to the hand order. The downbeats (1, 2, 3, and 4) will be played with one hand, while the upbeats (the *and*'s) will be played with the other hand. Practice each staff individually and slowly.

SOLO 3

(Eighth Notes and Rests)

Track 14

IMPORTANT: Count aloud. Practice each staff individually. Pay attention to the hand order. Play through without stopping.

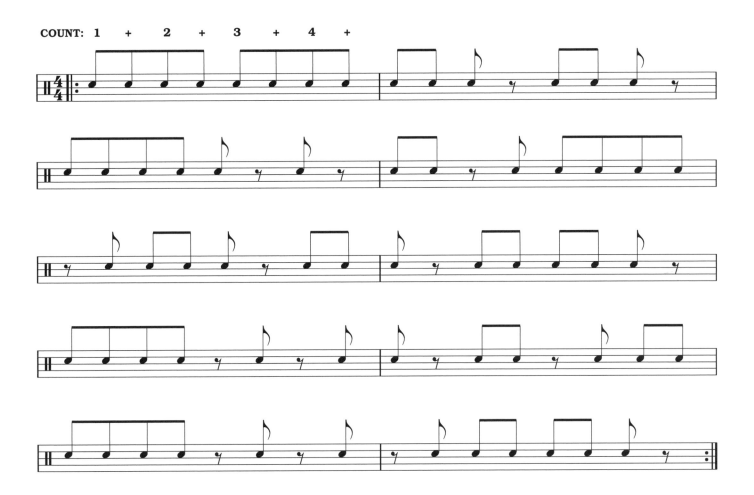

NOTES:

QUARTER AND EIGHTH NOTES

Track 15

(with Rests)

IMPORTANT: **Don't forget to count during the rests. Pay attention to the hand order. Play slowly.**

SOLO 4

(with Quarter and Eighth Rests)

Track 16

IMPORTANT: Play through the whole exercise without stopping. Pay attention to the hand order. Don't forget to count during the rests.

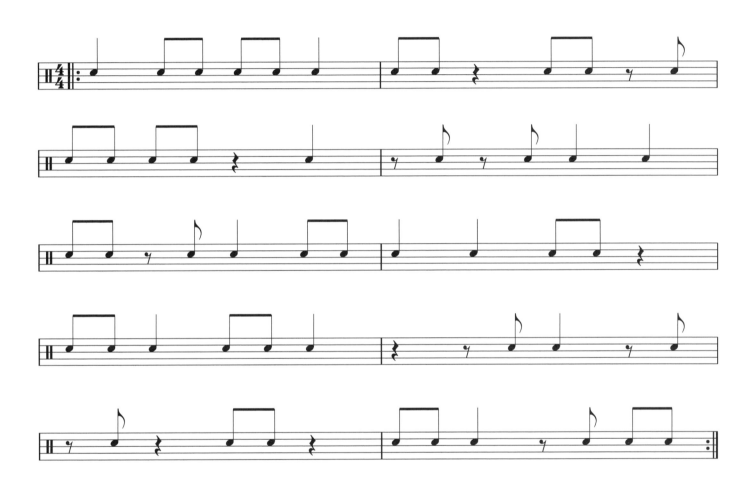

NOTES:

EIGHTH-NOTE GROOVES

(with Rests)

Track 17

IMPORTANT: This exercise stresses the importance of reading rests, which are used here to create syncopated rhythms. The right hand can accompany on either the hi-hat or the ride cymbal. Play slowly. Count aloud.

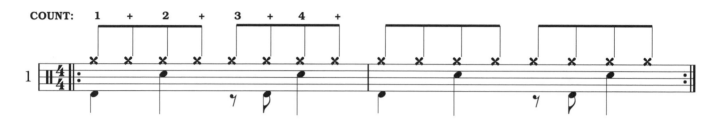

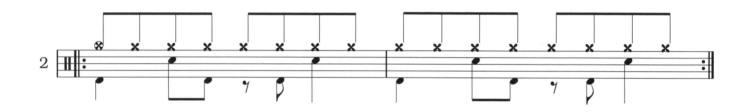

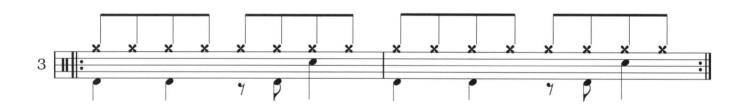

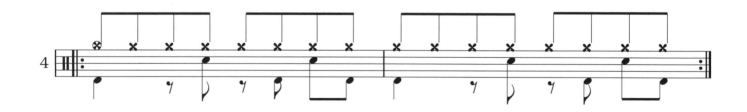

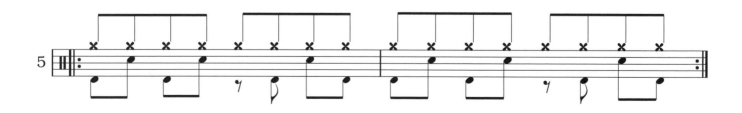

SOLO 4.1

(on the Drums)

Track 18

IMPORTANT: **This solo focuses on a persistent eighth-note flow. Keep a steady tempo. Play slowly. Play through from beginning to end.**

23

SIXTEENTH NOTES

(on the Pad)

Track 19

IMPORTANT: Sixteenth notes divide a ⁴⁄₄ bar into sixteen parts (in other words, four subdivisions to each quarter note). When dealing with sixteenth notes, all the downbeats and *and*'s should be played with the right hand and all the *e*'s and *a*'s with the left hand. Count sixteenth-note passages like this: "1 e + a, 2 e + a, 3 e + a, 4 e + a, *etc.*" Play slowly at first. Count aloud.

COUNT: 1 e + a 2 e + a 3 e + a 4 e + a

SOLO 5

(on the Pad)

Track 20

IMPORTANT: **Don't forget to count during the rests. Play slowly at first. Pay attention to the hand order.**

NOTES:

FILLS ON THE DRUMS
(Sixteenth Notes)

Track 21

IMPORTANT: This exercise should be practiced in the same way as the eighth-note fills from earlier in the book. The hand order is the same as in the previous sixteenth-note exercises. This exercise should be practiced with the hands at first. Later, try adding various rhythms with the bass drum or hi-hat pedal to provide counterpoint and interest. For example, take each one-bar pattern on this page and play it over the rhythms found on page 20, which can be played with the feet.

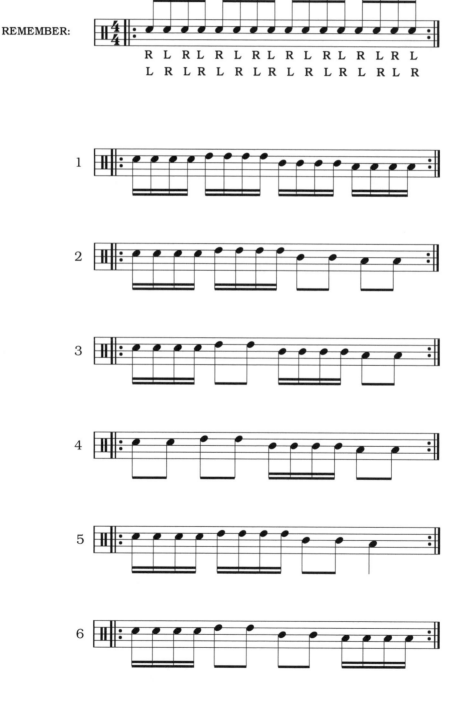

FILLS WITH CRASH CYMBAL

(Sixteenth Notes)

Track 22

IMPORTANT: The crash cymbal must be played exactly together with the bass drum. It is very important to count aloud and play slowly at first.

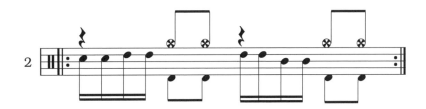

NOTES:

GROOVES AND FILLS

(Sixteenth Notes)

IMPORTANT: Now we will combine eighth-note grooves with sixteenth-note fills, which requires a change of subdivision when counting. The grooves and fills are played without any pauses between them. Play slowly at first. Count aloud. Each groove should be accompanied once on the hi-hat and once on the ride cymbal.

SOLO 5.1

(on the Drums)

Track 24

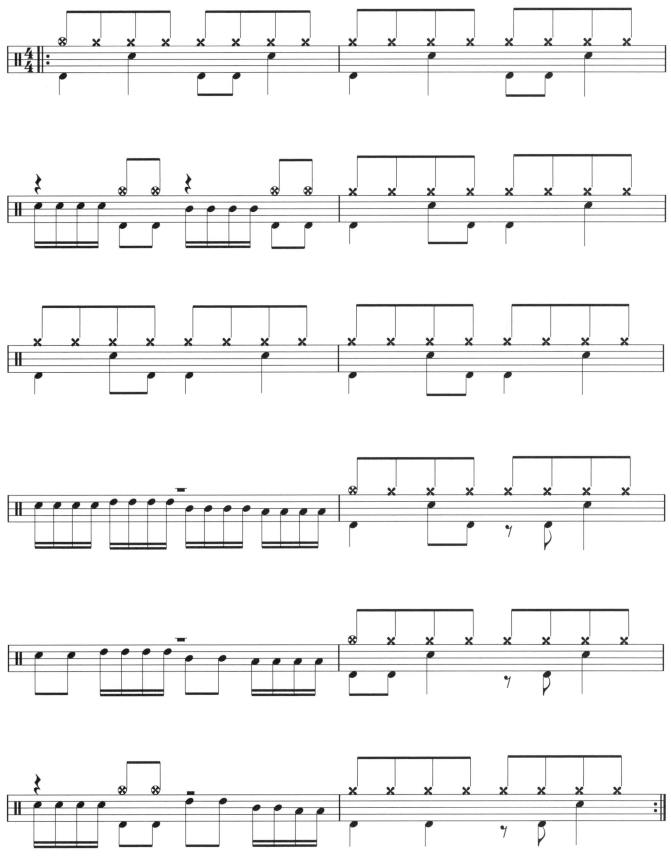

SIXTEENTH NOTES

(Figure A)

Track 25

IMPORTANT: It is very important to pay attention to the hand order in these exercises. Count using sixteenth-note subdivisions. Play slowly at first. Practice each staff individually.

SOLO 6

(on the Pad)

Track 26

IMPORTANT: Remember to count during the rests. Pay attention to your hand order. Play the entire solo without stopping.

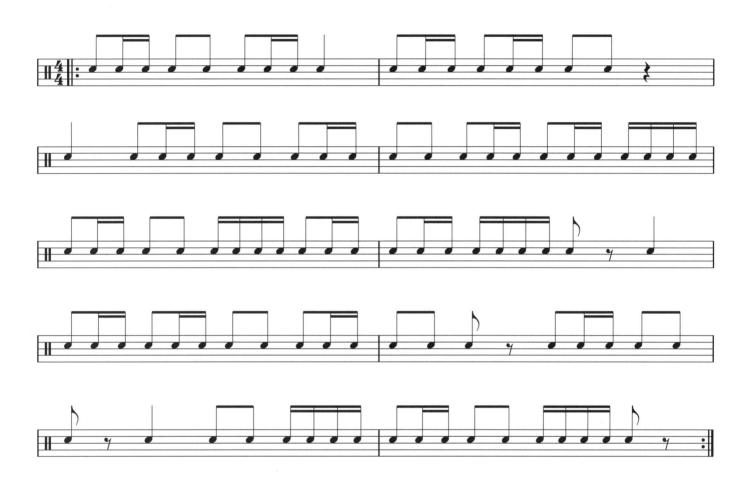

___

NOTES:

FILLS ON THE DRUMS

(Sixteenth-Note—Figure A)

Track 27

IMPORTANT: This exercise should be played with the hands (no feet) at first. Play slowly at first. After you feel comfortable with the grooves, try the superimposition idea mentioned on page 26.

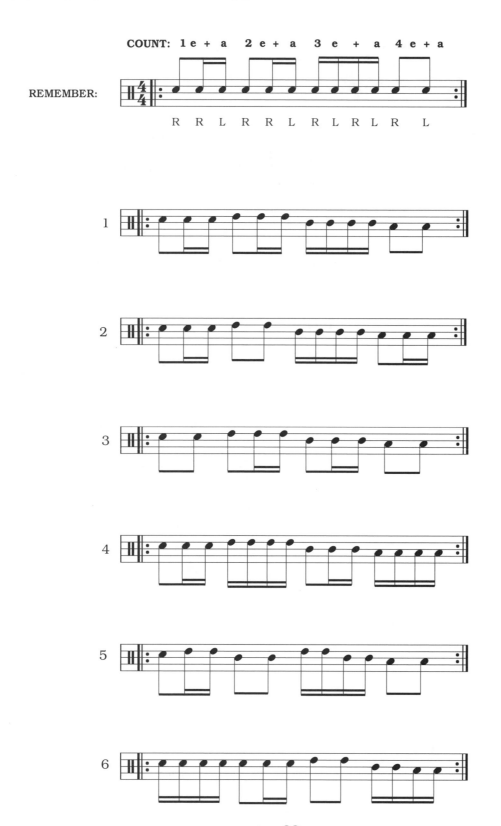

32

FILLS WITH CRASH CYMBAL

(Sixteenth-Note—Figure A)

Track 28

IMPORTANT: The crash cymbal must be played exactly together with the bass drum. It is very important to count aloud and to practice slowly at first.

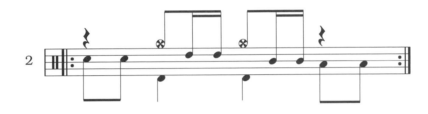

NOTES:

GROOVES AND FILLS

(Sixteenth-Note—Figure A)

Track 29

IMPORTANT: Now we are going to combine eighth-note grooves with the new sixteenth-note figure incorporated in the fills. The grooves and fills should be played continuously, without pausing. Pay attention to the hand order. All exercises should be accompanied once with the hi-hat and once with the ride cymbal.

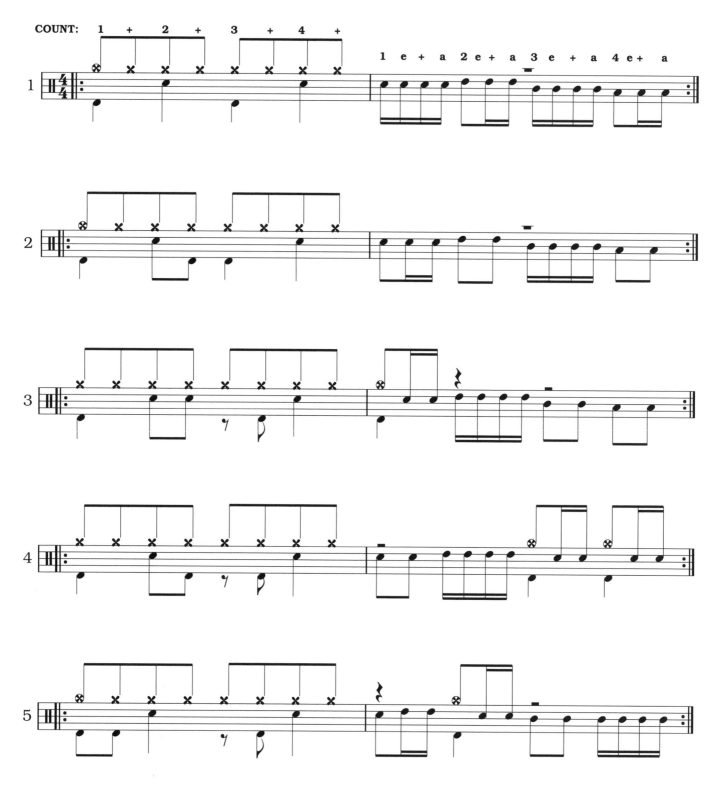

SOLO 6.1

(on the Drums)

SIXTEENTH NOTES

(Sixteenth-Note—Figure B)

Track 31

IMPORTANT: This figure also requires you to count using sixteenth-note subdivisions. Play slowly at first. Pay attention to the hand order.

SOLO 7
(Figure B)

Track 32

IMPORTANT: Don't stop counting during the rests. Pay attention to the hand order.

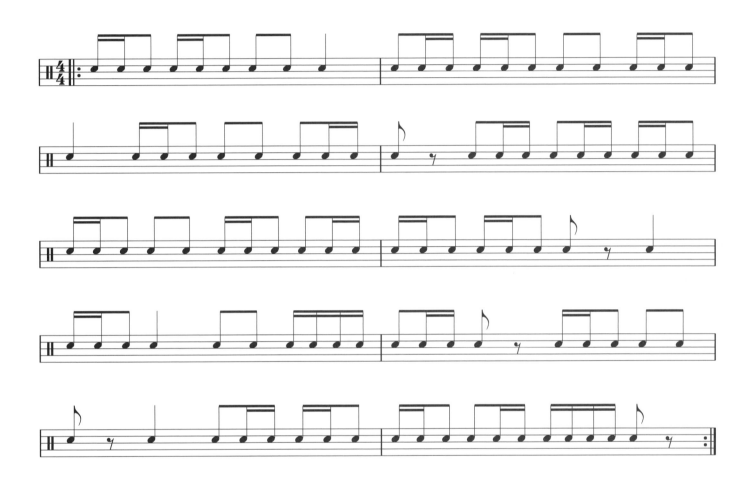

NOTES:

FILLS ON THE DRUMS

(Sixteenth-Note—Figure B)

Track 33

IMPORTANT: The hand order is very important in this exercise. Again, try out the superimposition idea mentioned on page 26.

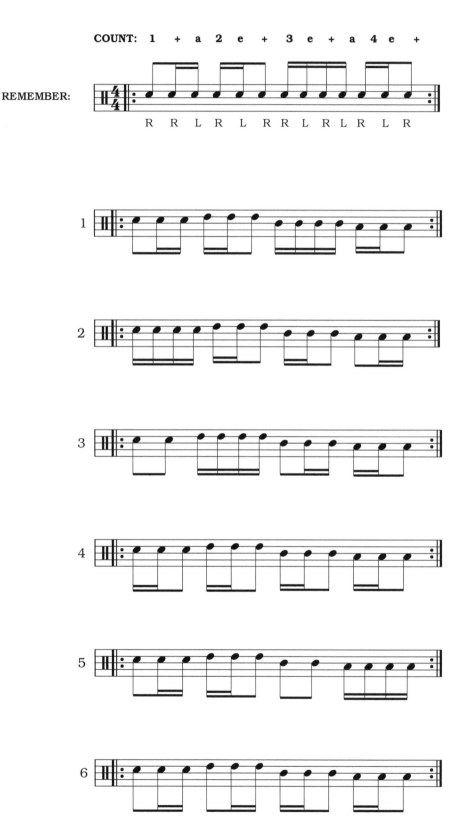

38

FILLS WITH CRASH CYMBAL

(Sixteenth-Note—Figure B)

Track 34

IMPORTANT: **The crash cymbal must be played exactly together with the bass drum. It is very important to count aloud and play slowly at first.**

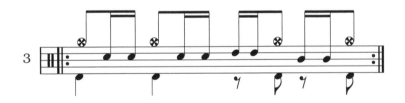

NOTES:

39

GROOVES AND FILLS

(Sixteenth-Note—Figure B)

Track 35

IMPORTANT: The fills in this exercise present the two new sixteenth-note figures in combinations. Grooves and fills should be played without pauses between them. Pay attention to the hand order. Count aloud. Play slowly at first.

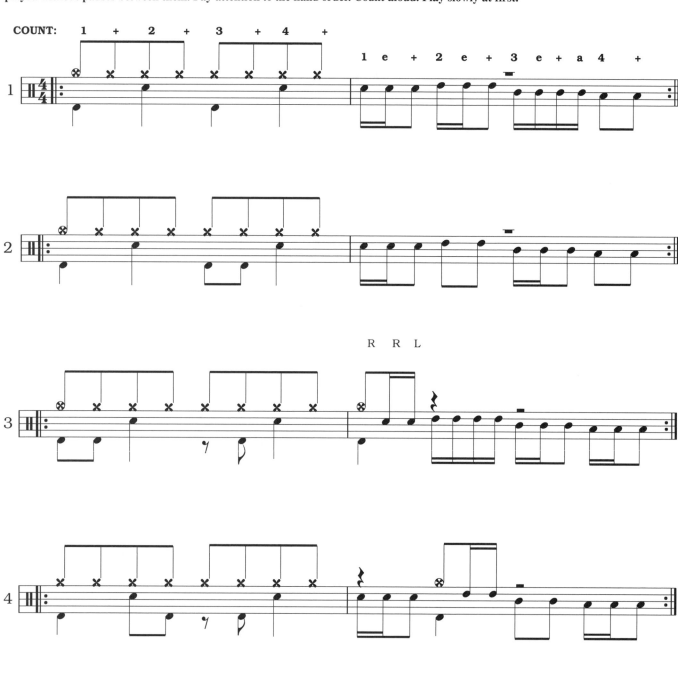

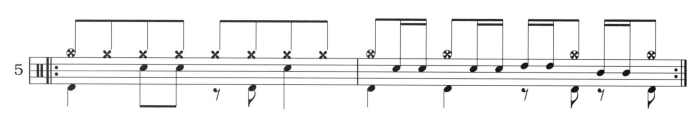

SOLO 7.1

(on the Drums)

Track 36

IMPORTANT: Keep a slow, steady tempo and play through the whole solo without stopping. Don't forget about the hand order.

PART 2

DOTTED NOTES

(Explanation)

IMPORTANT: A dot makes a note last 50 percent longer. For example, a dotted half note is worth three beats—the half note's two beats plus 50 percent of its value, a quarter note. The dot makes the page look less busy, because fewer rests are required. Drums are only capable of sustaining long tones by using rolls, which is the only case where a dot actually retains its true meaning.

Dotted Half Notes:

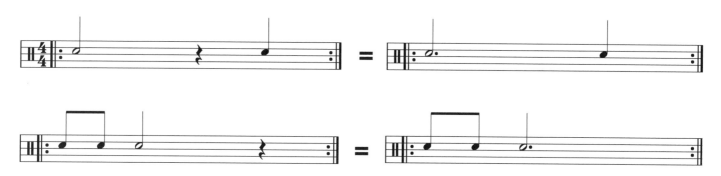

Dotted Quarter Notes:

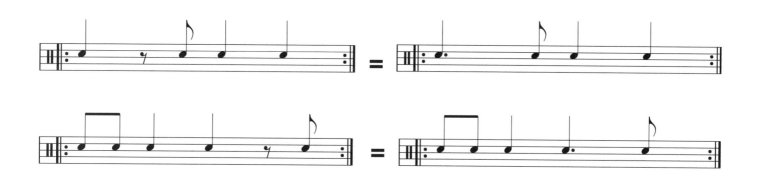

Dotted Eighth Notes:

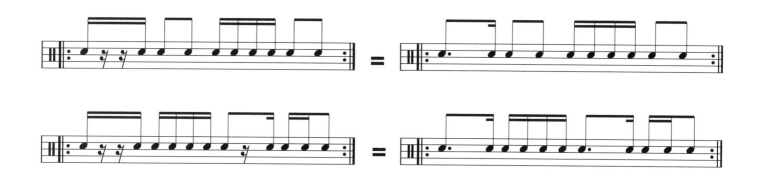

43

DOTTED NOTES

(on the Pad)

Track 37

IMPORTANT: The following reading exercise shows various rhythms written differently, but played in the same way—which demonstrates that a dotted note has the same sound as a note-and-rest combination in drumming. Practice each staff individually and count aloud. Pay attention to your hand order: all *e* and *a* counts should be played with the left hand.

COUNT: 1 e + a 2 e + a 3 + 4 +

44

SOLO 8

(Dotted Notes)

IMPORTANT: Remember to count during the rests. Play slowly at first. Pay attention to the hand order. Play through without stopping.

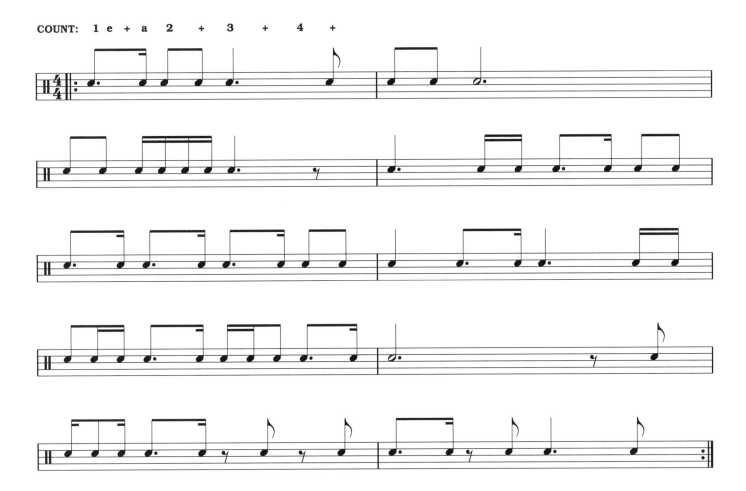

COUNT: 1 e + a 2 + 3 + 4 +

NOTES:

RHYTHMS

(with Accented Sixteenth Notes)

Track 39

IMPORTANT: In this exercise, the sixteenth-note subdivisions should be counted aloud. Play slowly so that the bass drum and snare drum rhythms are precise. The hi-hat's eighth notes must be played steadily and evenly. All rhythms should be accompanied once on the hi-hat and once on the ride cymbal. Play slowly at first. Practice each staff individually.

COUNT: 1 e + a 2 e + a 3 e + a 4 e + a

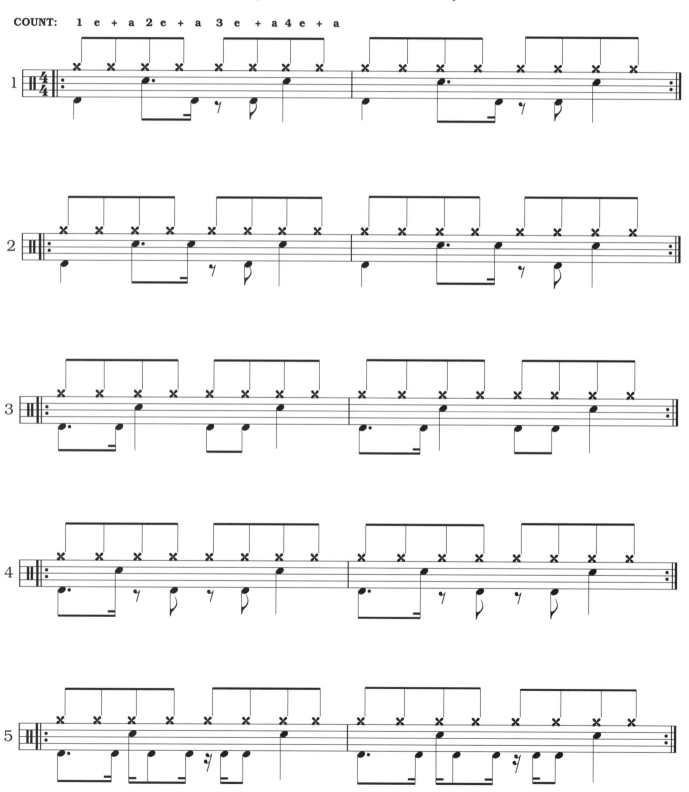

SIXTEENTH-NOTE GROOVES

Track 40

IMPORTANT: The sixteenth-note subdivisions should be clearly counted aloud. Play slowly so that the accents can be exactly placed on the bass drum or on the snare drum. Both hands should be played on the hi-hat (hand-to-hand). It is important to note, with regard to the bass drum hits, that the hi-hat and the bass drum are played exactly together.

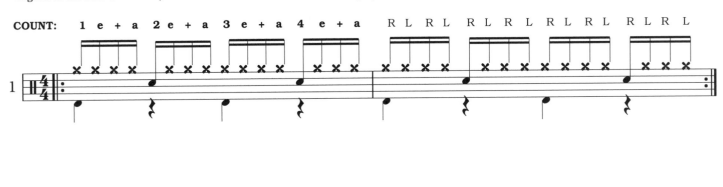

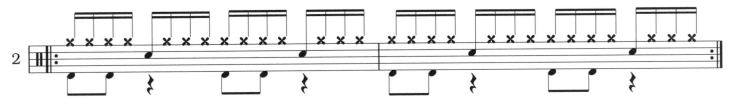

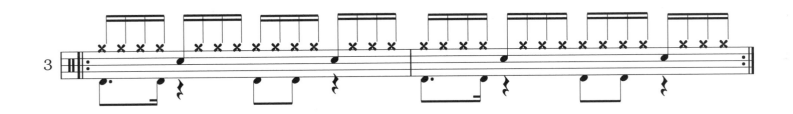

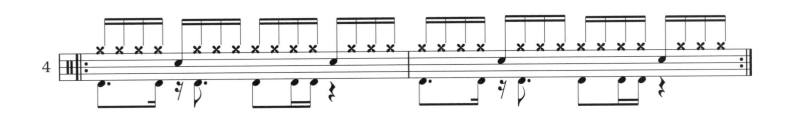

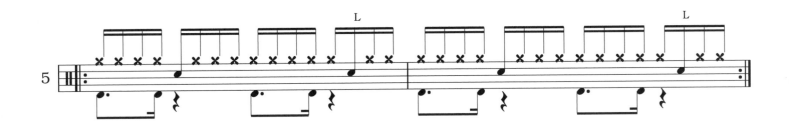

OPEN ROLLS

(on the Pad)

Track 41

IMPORTANT: The open roll is an important technique that, with exacting diligent and consistent practice, will open a big door into the art of drumming. The open roll requires a precise *stick control* technique, which dictates that each stroke should be played equally loud and that wrist strokes are used for each articulation. When you increase the tempo, begin to implement a bounce to articulate the second stroke of each hand. This exercise should be practiced thoroughly in order to optimize its benefits.

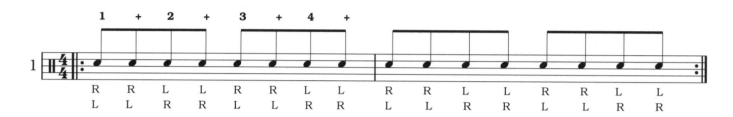

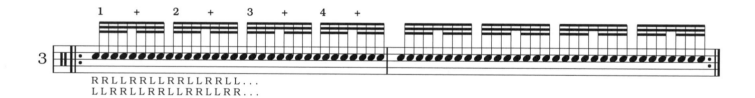

SIMPLIFIED FORM OF WRITING:

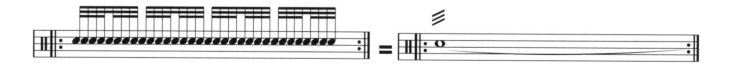

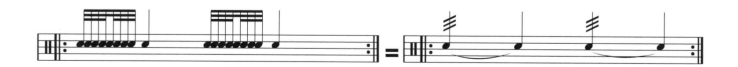

GROOVES AND FILLS

(with Open Rolls)

Track 42

IMPORTANT: Here, eighth-note grooves are combined with open rolls. When practicing these exercises, each stroke should be equally loud and should in no way be "pressed." Rolls should always be included in a student's daily warm-up routine.

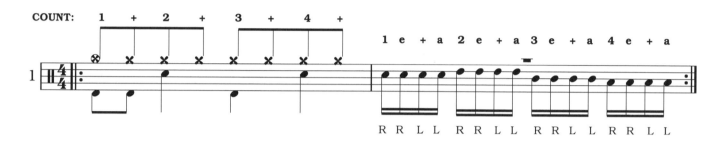

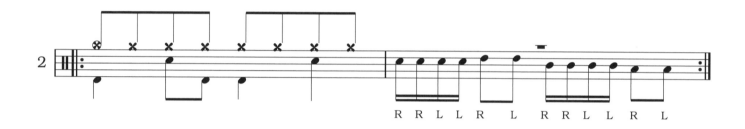

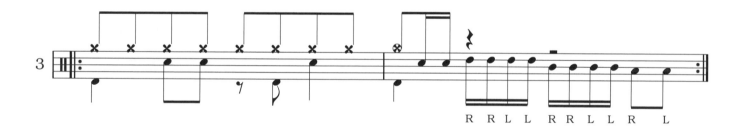

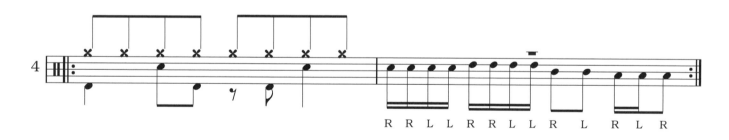

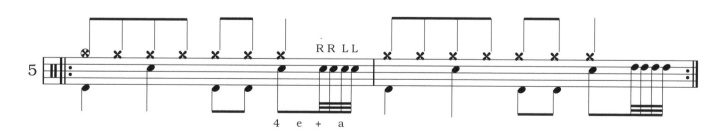

PARADIDDLES

(on the Pad)

IMPORTANT: The single paradiddle is a fixed sticking sequence that can be used in a variety of ways. At first, it is very important to verbalize the sticking while you play: "right-left-right-right, left-right-left-left." If you can play the paradiddle quickly, and by heart, on the pad, it will be a lot easier when you play it on the drums later.

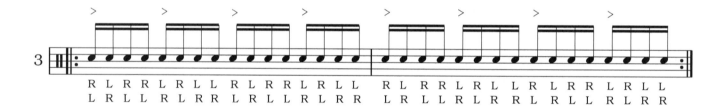

NOTES:

FILLS ON THE DRUMS

(with Paradiddles)

Track 44

IMPORTANT: Here, the paradiddle is applied to the drums. The paradiddle sticking (hand order) is used throughout all six exercises.

GROOVES AND FILLS

(with Paradiddles)

Track 45

IMPORTANT: Each of these exercises begins with an eighth-note groove followed by a paradiddle-based fill. Again, the sticking remains the same in every exercise. Play each staff individually and accompany each once with the hi-hat and once with the ride cymbal.

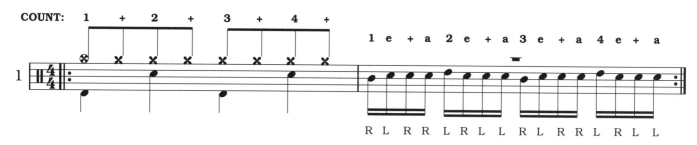

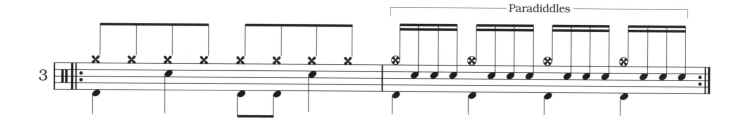

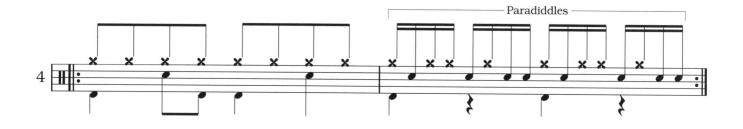

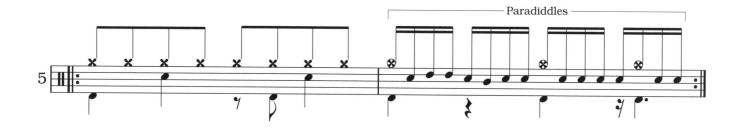

SOLO 9.1

(on the Drums)

Track 46

IMPORTANT: Keep the tempo steady. Play slowly at first. Play each staff alone, and then play the whole page continuously.

SIXTEENTH NOTES

(Reading and Hand-Order Exercise)

Track 47

IMPORTANT: This is a reading and hand-order exercise. While you are counting "1 e + a, 2 e + a, 3 e + a, 4 e + a, *etc.*," make sure that every *e* and *a* is played with the left hand. Practice each staff individually. Play slowly at first.

SOLO 10

(on the Pad)

Track 48

IMPORTANT: Continue counting during the rests. Pay attention to the sticking. Play through the whole solo without stopping. Keep a steady tempo.

<u>**NOTES:**</u>

EIGHTH-NOTE TRIPLETS

(on the Pad)

Track 49

IMPORTANT: Eighth-note triplets divide a $\frac{4}{4}$ bar into twelve parts (in other words, three subdivisions to each quarter note). When we play triplets, the hand order for the downbeats alternates; in other words, if we start with the right hand on beat 1, the left hand plays on beat 2, and so on. Count like this: "1 trip-let, 2 trip-let, 3 trip-let, 4 trip-let, *etc.*" Play each staff individually.

SOLO 11

(on the Pad)

Track 50

IMPORTANT: Keep a steady tempo. Count aloud. Play through the whole solo without stopping.

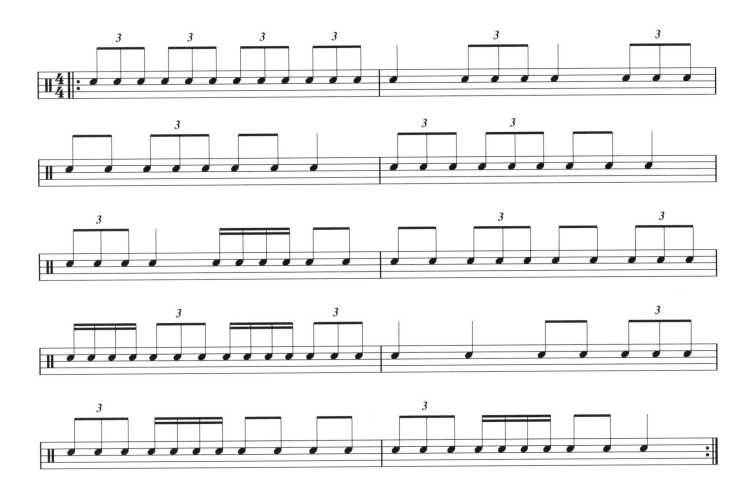

NOTES:

FILLS ON THE DRUMS

(Eighth-Note Triplets)

Track 51

IMPORTANT: These exercises should be played with the hands until you are comfortable, then try adding various rhythms with the feet. Be careful when placing triplets over eighth notes—this is the realm of polyrhythms!

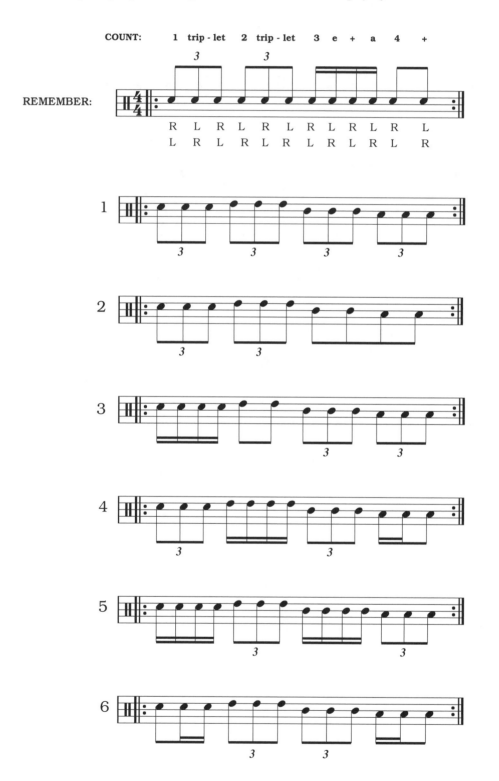

FILLS WITH CRASH CYMBAL

(Eighth-Note Triplets)

Track 52

IMPORTANT: **Play slowly at first. The crash cymbal should be played exactly together with the bass drum. Watch the hand order in Ex. 2. Always play hand-to-hand.**

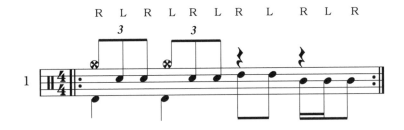

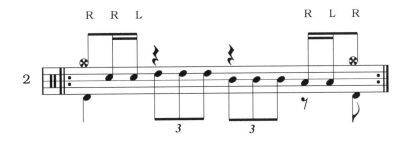

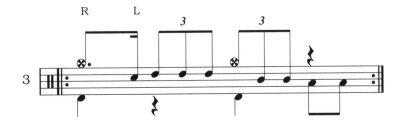

NOTES:

GROOVES AND FILLS

(Eighth-Note Triplets)

Track 53

IMPORTANT: Eighth-note grooves are combined with eighth-note triplet fills; this requires a subdivision shift when counting. Make sure there is no pause between the grooves and fills. All exercises should be accompanied once with the hi-hat and once with the ride cymbal. Play slowly at first. Count aloud.

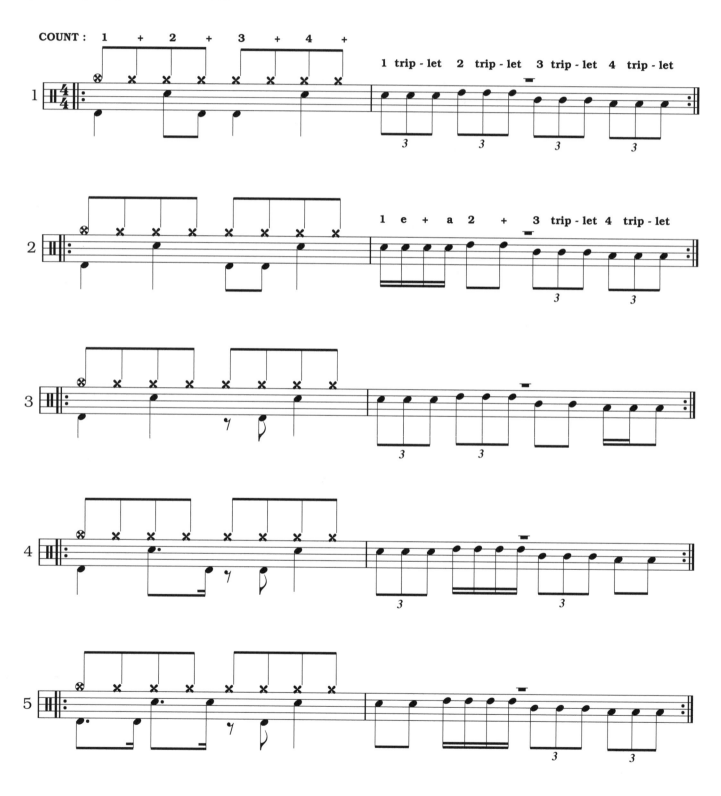

SOLO 11.1

(on the Drums)

Track 54

IMPORTANT: **Keep a steady tempo. Play through the entire solo without stopping. Count aloud.**

SIXTEENTH-NOTE TRIPLETS

(on the Pad)

Track 55

IMPORTANT: Sixteenth-note triplets divide a 4/4 bar into 24 parts (in other words, six subdivisions to each quarter note). The hand order is still hand-to-hand: R L R, L R L, *etc.* Count "1 trip-let + trip-let, 2 trip-let + trip-let, 3 trip-let + trip-let, 4 trip-let + trip-let, *etc.*"

SOLO 12

(on the Pad)

IMPORTANT: Play slowly at first. Play through without stopping.

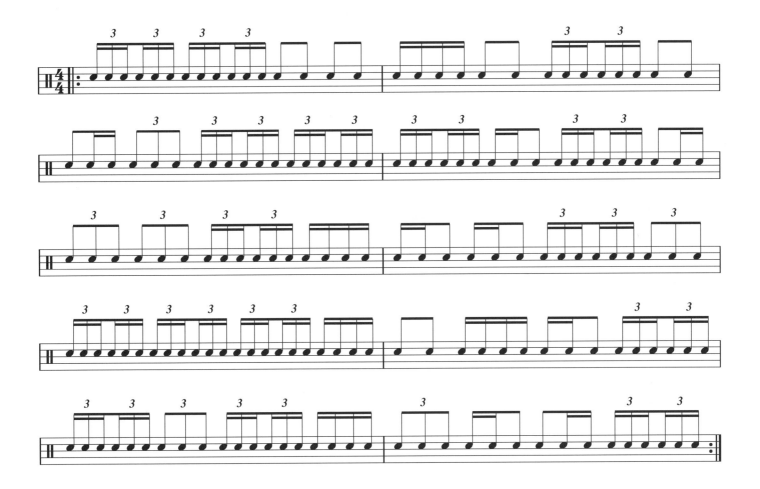

NOTES:

FILLS ON THE DRUMS

(Sixteenth-Note Triplets)

Track 57

IMPORTANT: Counting aloud will make the exercises easier. Play slowly at first.

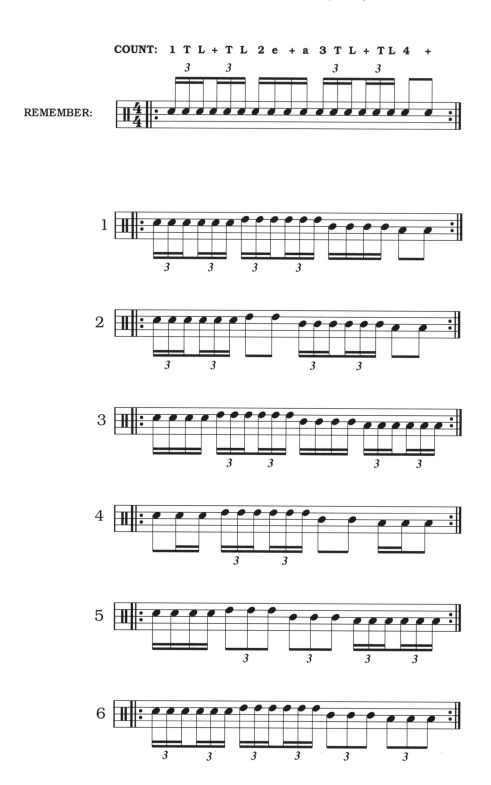

64

FILLS WITH CRASH CYMBAL

(Sixteenth-Note Triplets)

Track 58

IMPORTANT: The crash cymbal must be played exactly together with the bass drum. It is very important to count aloud and play slowly.

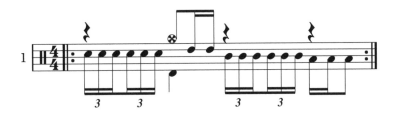

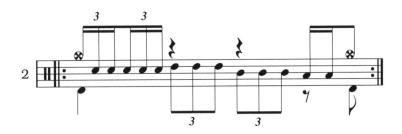

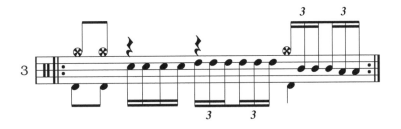

NOTES:

65

GROOVES AND FILLS

(Sixteenth-Note Triplets)

Track 59

IMPORTANT: Eighth-note grooves are combined with sixteenth-note triplet fills. There should be no pause between the grooves and fills. Work on each staff individually at first. All exercises should be accompanied once with the hi-hat and once with the ride cymbal.

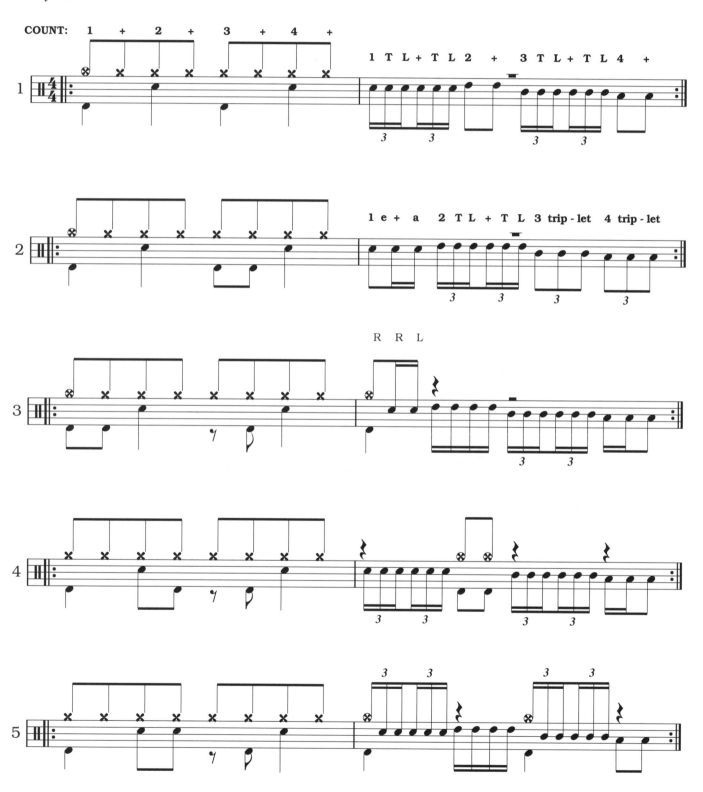

SOLO 12.1

(on the Drums)

Track 60

IMPORTANT: Keep a steady tempo. Play slowly at first. Play through without stopping.

COUNT: 1 e + a 2 + 3 T L + T L 4 +

67

SIXTEENTH-NOTE TRIPLETS

(Figure A)

Track 61

IMPORTANT: These exercises employ sixteenth-note triplet figures, but only during the first half of each beat, though you should count the sixteenth-note subdivisions throughout: "1 trip-let + trip-let, 2 trip-let + trip-let, 3 trip-let + trip-let, 4 trip-let + trip-let, *etc.*" Remember to play slowly at first.

SOLO 13

(on the Pad)

Track 62

IMPORTANT: Pay special attention to the subdivisions as you count. Play slowly at first.

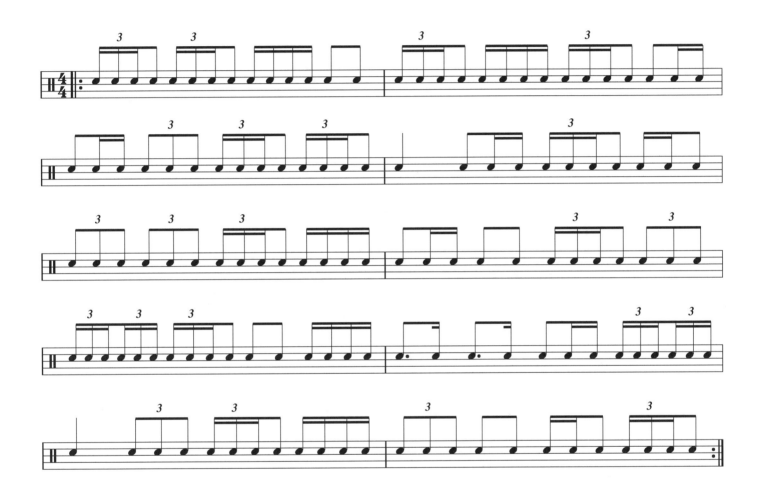

NOTES:

FILLS ON THE DRUMS

(Figure A)

Track 63

IMPORTANT: Counting aloud will make these exercises easier. Play slowly at first.

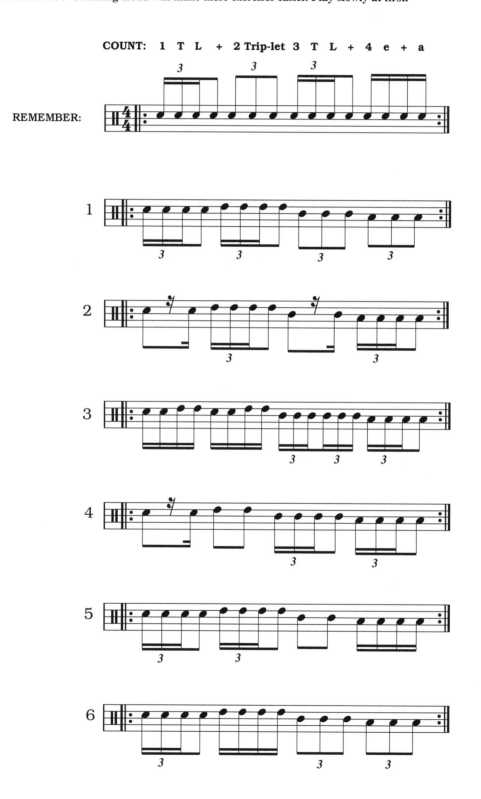

FILLS WITH CRASH CYMBAL

(Figure A)

Track 64

IMPORTANT: The crash cymbal must be played exactly together with the bass drum. It is very important to count aloud and to play slowly when learning these exercises.

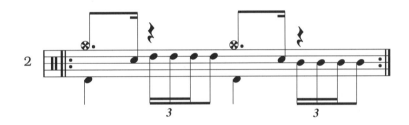

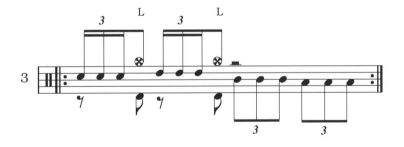

NOTES:

GROOVES AND FILLS

(Figure A)

Track 65

IMPORTANT: Eighth-note grooves are combined with sixteenth-note triplet fills in the following exercises. Remember to play without any pause between the grooves and fills. Play each staff individually.

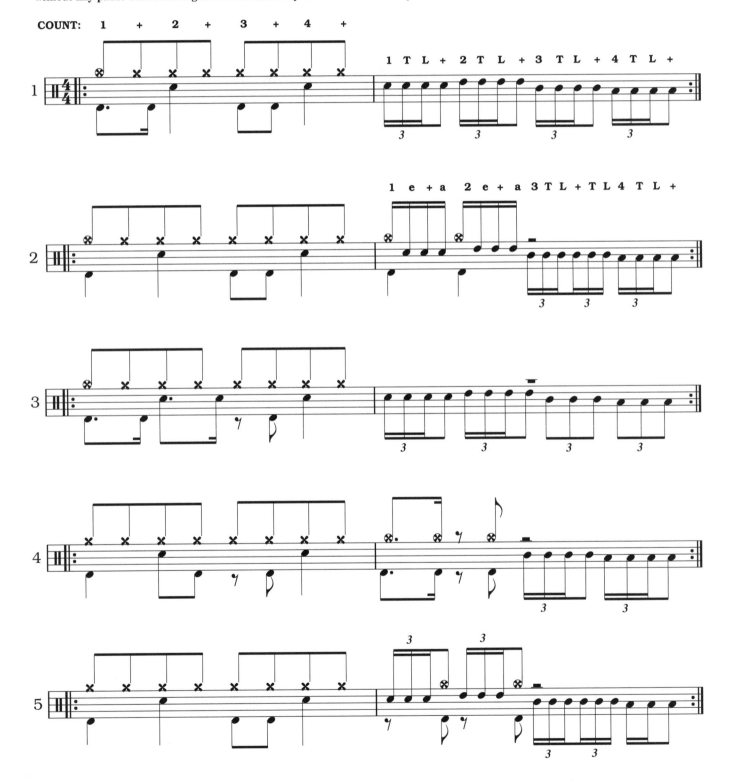

72

SOLO 13.1

(on the Drums)

Track 66

IMPORTANT: Keep a steady tempo. Play through without stopping.

SIXTEENTH-NOTE TRIPLETS

(Figure B)

Track 67

IMPORTANT: The hand order is crucial in these sixteenth-note triplet exercises. Play each staff individually. Count aloud.

SOLO 14

(on the Pad)

IMPORTANT: Play slowly at first. Count aloud. Play through without stopping.

NOTES:

FILLS ON THE DRUMS

(Figure B)

IMPORTANT: Counting aloud will help. Play slowly at first.

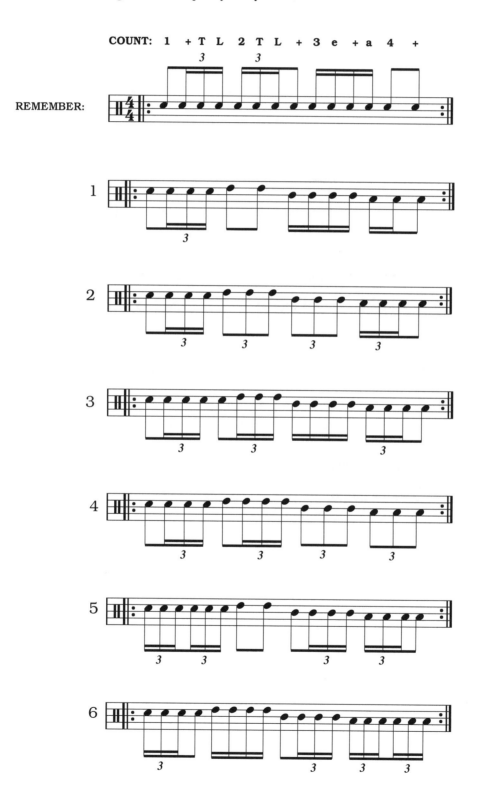

FILLS WITH CRASH CYMBAL

(Figure B)

Track 70

IMPORTANT: The crash cymbal must be played exactly together with the bass drum. It is very important to count aloud and to play slowly when you first start learning these exercises.

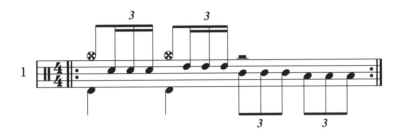

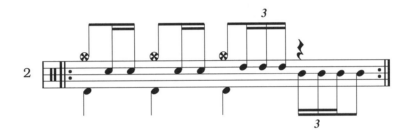

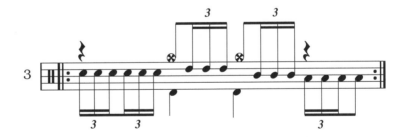

NOTES:

GROOVES AND FILLS

(Figure B)

Track 71

IMPORTANT: Here, eighth-note grooves are combined with various sixteenth-note triplet fills. The grooves and fills should be played without any pause between them. Play slowly at first. Pay attention to the hand order.

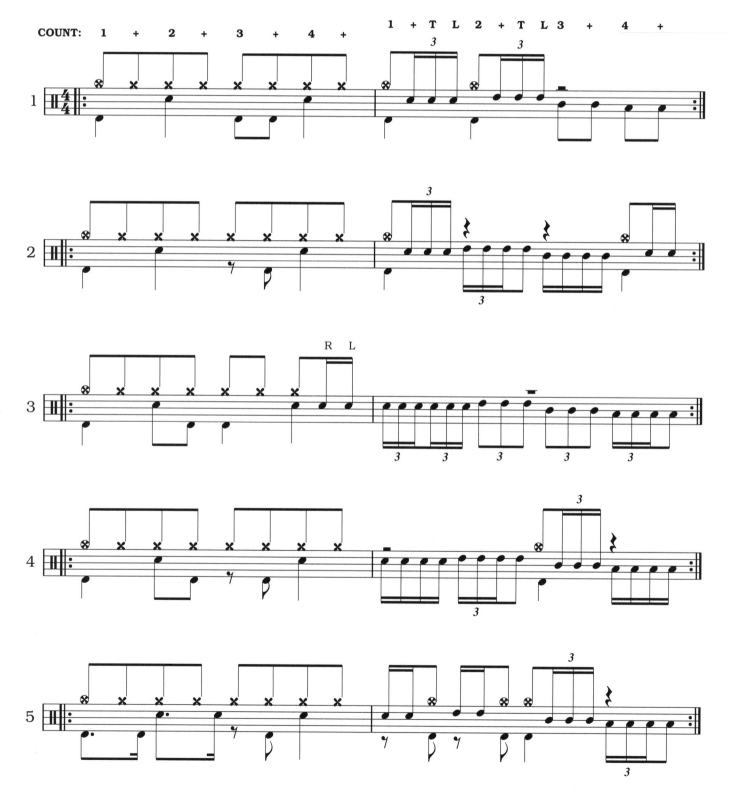

SOLO 14.1

(on the Drums)

Track 72

IMPORTANT: Keep a steady tempo. Play through the entire solo without stopping.

79

SOLO 15

(on the Drums)

Track 73

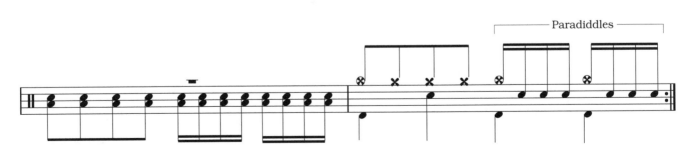

SOLO 16

(on the Drums)

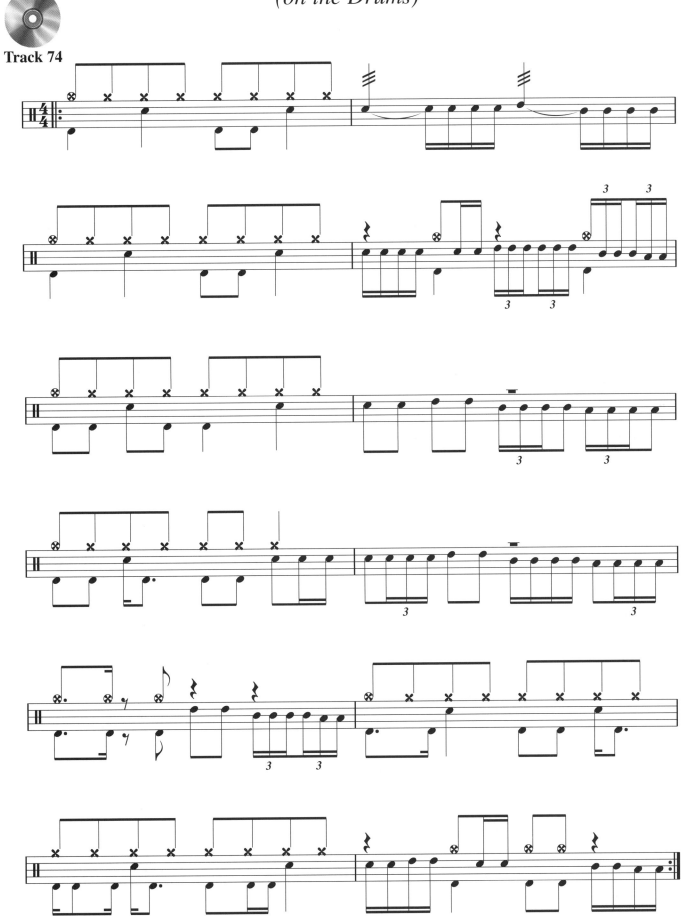

SOLO 17
(on the Drums)

SOLO 18

(on the Drums)

SOLO 19

(on the Drums)

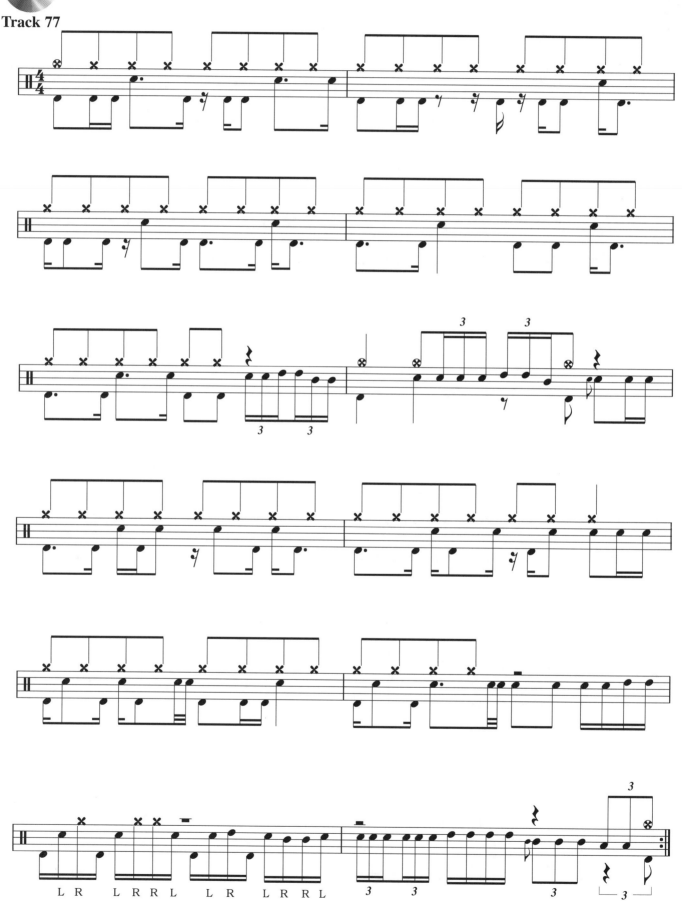

SOLO 20

(on the Drums)

WRITING EXERCISES

(for drum solo notation)

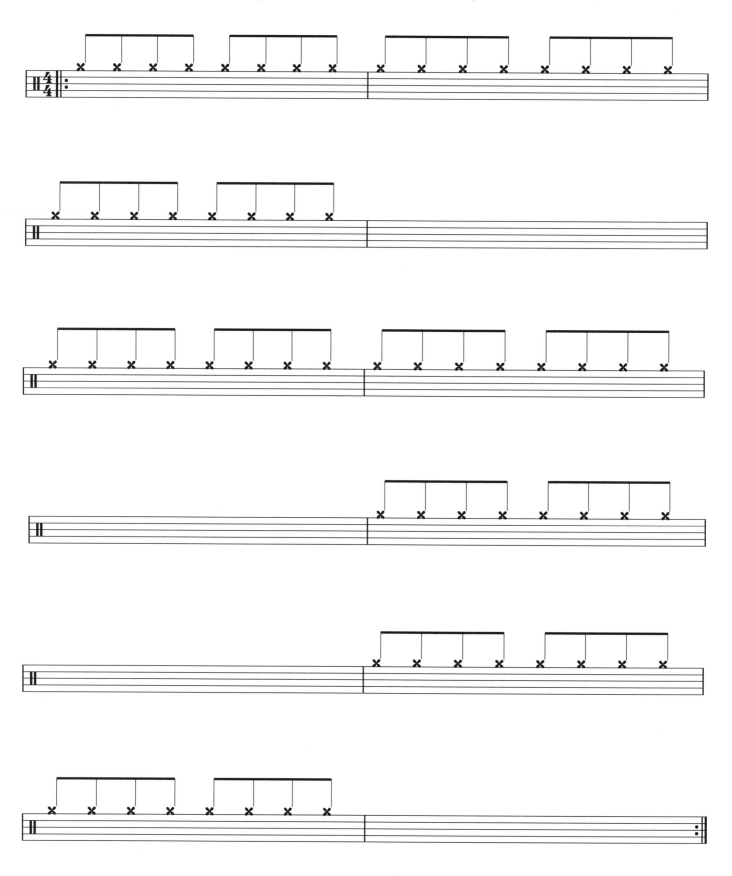

86

NOTES